Elizabeth Ann Chase Akers Allen

The High-Top Sweeting

And Other Poems

Elizabeth Ann Chase Akers Allen

The High-Top Sweeting
And Other Poems

ISBN/EAN: 9783744649209

Printed in Europe, USA, Canada, Australia, Japan

Cover: Foto ©Thomas Meinert / pixelio.de

More available books at **www.hansebooks.com**

THE

HIGH-TOP SWEETING

And Other Poems

BY

ELIZABETH AKERS

NEW YORK
CHARLES SCRIBNER'S SONS
1891

Copyright, 1891,
By Charles Scribner's Sons.

University Press:
John Wilson and Son, Cambridge.

CONTENTS.

	PAGE
THE HIGH-TOP SWEETING	1
ODE TO APHRODITE (SAPPHO)	9
IN A GARRET	11
THE BOBOLINK	14
THE LAST LANDLORD	17
IF I SHOULD TELL YOU	20
LAURETTE	22
THE STONE-CUTTER	24
WIDOW AND ORPHAN	28
EVERY DAY	31
A SUMMER MELODY	34
THE LILAC-TREE. CHANT-ROYAL	36
THE SWEETEST SLEEP	39
HER LIFE LONG	43
FLOWERS IN RAIN	45
SOME DAY	47
COULD SUMMER LAST FOREVER	49

CONTENTS.

	PAGE
UNWEDDED	53
IN THE FIELDS	57
BEFORE DARK	61
A STRATFORD WILD-ROSE	63
FAITHFUL UNTO DEATH	66
TWO LIVES	69
O CRICKET, HUSH!	71
TEARS	74
OVER SEA	76
SOME HEARTS GO HUNGERING	80
LATE OCTOBER	82
"IN EVERY PORT"	85
A HYACINTH	91
SLIGHTED VALUES	94
FAITH AND SIGHT	96
AN OLD POET	97
A FORSAKEN FAVORITE	101
NATURE'S HEALERS	103
THE STORY OF KIDHZ	106
"A GARDEN ENCLOSED"	110
FOUR WORDS	113
ALWAYS A BABY	115
REST	118
THE CLAY CHERUB	120

CONTENTS.

	PAGE
APRIL AGAIN	124
THE FOG	126
LOYALTY	128
THE SWALLOWS	130
A WINTER GRAVE	133
THROUGH THE WHEAT	135
STORM	138
VACANT PLACES	139
A PILLOW OF ROSES	141

THE HIGH-TOP SWEETING.

TALLEST of all the orchard trees,
  Its boughs the greensward meeting,
Shading with greenest of canopies
The meadow bars, and the stand of bees,
It stood, with an air of sturdy ease,
As if it had waved for centuries,
Bounteous queen of the fruitful leas;
And the apples it swung in the sun and breeze
Might rival the fair Hesperides', —
  The dear old high-top sweeting!

Lovely it was when its blossoms came
  To answer the bluebird's greeting;
They were dainty and white as a maiden's fame,
And pink as the flush of tender shame
That lights her cheek at her lover's name;
And the place was bright with the rosy flame
  Of the beautiful high-top sweeting.

Smiling up to the smiling day,
  A marvel of bloom and sweetness,
Just one bountiful, vast bouquet,
The pride and glory of later May,
No brush could paint it, no pen portray
  Its perfect and rare completeness,

When down in the cedar-swamp, the crow
  Cawed to his croaking neighbor,
And, scoring the furrows to and fro,
With the heavy oxen, strong and slow,
Where later the ribboned corn would grow, —
While the redbreast followed in every row,
To hapless earth-worms a keen-eyed foe, —
The noisy ploughman cried, " Whoa-hishe-whoa !
Back, now, steady! haw, Bright ! haw, Snow !"
  Or whistled to cheer his labor.

The delicate petals faded slow,
  Their annual doom repeating;
And the sprouting grass, and the path below,
Were covered white with their fragrant snow,
Dancing and drifting to and fro ;
And almost ere they had vanished, lo !
The tiny apples began to grow
  On the boughs of the high-top sweeting.

Scarcely the curious sun peered through,
  In his hottest summer beating,
The heavy branches, so thick they grew;
We children played there, from dawn till dew,
Laughing and romping, a merry crew;
And if it rained, or a hail-storm blew,
Sheltered beneath it, we hardly knew;
And the sods were worn, and the wind-falls few
  Under the high-top sweeting.

The pleasant sounds of the rural day, —
  The crunch of the cattle eating,
In the barn near by, their noon-time hay;
The waiting horse's impatient neigh;
The catbird's call from the maple spray;
The sparrow warbling his roundelay;
The swallow's chirp from its nest of clay
Under the rafters; and far away,
The throb of the saw-mill, old and gray,
And the river's song, as it sought the bay, —
We heard them all, in our happy play
  Under the high-top sweeting:

The mournful lowing of mother-cows,
  And the weanling calf's entreating

From the paddock near, where he learned to
 browse;
The cackle of fowls among the mows;
The small soft talk from the martin-house;
The pigeon, cooing his tender vows
Beside his gentle and constant spouse;
And the singing wind in the swaying boughs
 Of the dear old high-top sweeting.

Many a playmate came to share
 The sports of our merry meeting:
Zigzag butterflies, many a pair,
Doubled and danced in the sunny air;
The yellow wasp was a visitor there;
The cricket chirped from his grassy lair;
Even the squirrel would sometimes dare
Look down upon us, with curious stare;
The bees plied fearless their honeyed care
Almost beside us, nor seemed aware
Of human presence; and when the glare
Of day was done, and the eve was fair,
The fireflies glimmered everywhere,
Like diamond-sparkles in beauty's hair,
 In the boughs of the high-top sweeting.

The humming-bird, with his gem-bright eye,
   Paused there, to sip the clover,
Or whizzed like a rifle-bullet by ;
The katydid, with its rasping dry,
Made forever the same reply,
Which laughing voices would still deny ;
And the beautiful four-winged dragon-fly
Darted among us, now low, now high,
And we sprang aside with a startled cry,
Fearing the fancied savagery
   Of the harmless and playful rover.

The flying grasshopper clacked his wings,
   Like castanets gayly beating ;
The toad hopped by us, with jolting springs ;
The yellow spider that spins and swings
Swayed on its ladder of silken strings ;
The shy cicada, whose noon-voice rings
So piercing-shrill that it almost stings
The sense of hearing, and all the things
Which the fervid northern summer brings, —
The world that buzzes and crawls and sings, —
   Were friends of the high-top sweeting.

The balsam lifted its coronal
   Of jewels, so fair and fleeting,

Worn as ear-drops, by damsels small,
At many a mimic festival;
And in late summer and early fall,
The gay rudbeckia nodded, to call
The bumblebee to her banquet-hall,
And golden-rod grew yellow and tall,
'Mid purple asters, more fair than all,
With the raspberry-briers, by the old stone wall
    Close by the high-top sweeting.

Late in August, the gracious sun,
    His pleasant task completing,
Smiled at the work so nearly done,
And reddened the apple-cheeks, every one,
With ripening kisses; and then begun
    Was the feast of the high-top sweeting.

The fruit, with its flavor wild and sweet,
    Was fit for a dryad's eating;
Scores of children, with eager feet,
Flocked beneath it, to pluck and eat;
And all the folk from the village street
Paused in passing, to taste the treat
    Of the generous high-top sweeting.

And now, is the tree that loved us so,
  Its summer tale repeating?
Or was its beautiful head laid low
By levelling tempests, long ago?
I cannot answer; but only know
That spring and summer will follow snow,
As changing seasons like billows flow,
But never another tree can grow
  So fair as the high-top sweeting!

Of the children who played beneath it then,
  In the days so bright and fleeting,
Some have vanished from mortal ken
Two brave boys of the nine or ten
Died in a Georgia prison-pen;
One in a Louisiana fen;
One starved, wandering in Darien;
One sleeps safe in her native glen;
The rest are grave-eyed women and men,
Wiser and sadder far than when
They played from sunrise till dark again
  Under the high-top sweeting.

Finer apples may redden and fall
  For happy children's eating,

But never a tree so brave and tall
Will grow, as that by the orchard wall,
The dear old tree that we used to call
The loveliest apple-tree of all, —
　The marvellous high-top sweeting!

ODE TO APHRODITE.

(SAPPHO.)

MIGHTY Queen of Love, deathless Aphrodite,
  Daughter of great Zeus, weaver of enchantments,
Torture not my heart with distress and anguish!
            Hear me, I pray thee!

Oh, come hither now, if thou heardst me ever
Calling on thy name, and didst deign to listen,
Leaving thy august father's golden mansion
            At my entreating.

To thy chariot yoked, fair fleet sparrows drew thee,
Flapping fast their wings; round the dark earth circling,
From the lofty heaven down through middle ether
            Quickly descending.

And thou, blessed one, smiling and immortal,
Didst thus question me, " Wherefore dost thou call
 me?
Whom does thy mad heart now desire to love thee?
   Who slights thee, Sappho?

"Ev'n though now he flies, he shall soon pursue
 thee;
Though he slights thy gifts, he shall bring thee
 many;
If he loves thee not, yet he soon shall love thee,
   Though now unwilling."

Hark to my appeal! from my grief release me,
All my heart desires, in thy might accomplish;
Be thou my ally in my need and weakness!
   Help me, O goddess!

IN A GARRET.

THIS realm is sacred to the silent past;
  Within its drowsy shades are treasures rare
Of dust and dreams; the years are long since last
  A stranger's footfall pressed the creaking stair.

This room no housewife's tidy hand disturbs;
  And here, like some strange presence, ever clings
A homesick smell of dry forgotten herbs,—
  A musty odor as of mouldering things.

Here stores of withered roots and leaves repose,
  For fancied virtues prized, in days of yore,
Gathered with thoughtful care, mayhap by those
  Whose earthly ills are healed forevermore.

Here shy Arachne winds her endless thread,
  And weaves her silken tapestry unseen,
Veiling the rough-hewn timbers overhead,
  And looping gossamer festoons between.

Along the low joists of the sloping roof,
    Moth-eaten garments hang, a gloomy row,
Like tall fantastic ghosts, which stand aloof,
    Holding grim converse with the long ago.

Here lie remembrancers of childish joys, —
    Old fairy-volumes, conned and conned again,
A cradle, and a heap of battered toys,
    Once loved by babes who now are bearded men.

Here, in the summer, at a broken pane,
    The yellow wasps come in, and buzz and build
Among the rafters; wind and snow and rain
    All enter, as the seasons are fulfilled.

This mildewed chest behind the chimney, holds
    Old letters, stained and nibbled; faintly show
The faded phrases on the tattered folds
    Once kissed, perhaps, or tear-wet — who may know?

I turn a page like one who plans a crime,
    And lo! love's prophecies and sweet regrets,
A tress of chestnut hair, a love-lorn rhyme,
    And fragrant dust that once was violets.

I wonder if the small sleek mouse, that shaped
   His winter nest between these time-stained beams,
Was happier that his bed was lined and draped
   With the bright warp and woof of youthful dreams?

Here where the gray incessant spiders spin,
   Shrouding from view the sunny world outside,
A golden bumblebee has blundered in
   And lost the way to liberty, and died.

So the lost present drops into the past;
   So the warm living heart, that loves the light,
Faints in the unresponsive darkness vast
   Which hides time's buried mysteries from sight.

Why rob these shadows of their sacred trust?
   Let the thick cobwebs hide the day once more;
Leave the dead years to silence and to dust,
   And close again the long unopened door.

THE BOBOLINK.

ONCE, on a golden afternoon,
    With radiant faces and hearts in tune,
Two fond lovers, in dreaming mood,
Threaded a rural solitude.
Wholly happy, they only knew
That the earth was bright and the sky was blue;
    That light and beauty and joy and song
    Charmed the way as they passed along.
The air was fragrant with woodland scents;
The squirrel frisked on the roadside fence;
    And hovering near them, "*Chee, chee, chink?*"
    Queried the curious bobolink,
Pausing and peering with sidelong head,
As saucily questioning all they said;
    While the ox-eye danced on its slender stem,
    And all glad Nature rejoiced with them.

Over the odorous fields were strown
Wilting windrows of grass new-mown;

And rosy billows of clover-bloom
Surged in the sunshine and breathed perfume.
Swinging low on a slender limb,
The sparrow warbled his wedding-hymn;
And balancing on a blackberry brier,
The bobolink sang with his heart on fire,
"*Chink? if you wish to kiss her, do!
Do it! do it! you coward, you!
Kiss her! kiss, kiss her! who will see?
Only we three! we three! we three!*"

Under garlands of drooping vines,
Through dim vistas of sweet-breathed pines,
Past wide meadow-fields, lately mowed,
Wandered the indolent country road.
The lovers followed it, listening still,
And, loitering slowly, as lovers will,
Entered a gray-roofed bridge, that lay
Dusk and cool, in their pleasant way.
Under its arch a smooth brown stream
Silently glided with glint and gleam,
Shaded by graceful elms which spread
Their verdurous canopy overhead, —
The stream so narrow, the boughs so wide,
They met and mingled across the tide.

Alders loved it, and seemed to keep
Patient watch as it lay asleep,
   Mirroring clearly the trees and sky,
   And the flitting form of the dragon-fly,
      Save where the swift-winged swallows played
      In and out in the sun and shade,
And darting and circling in merry chase,
Dipped, and dimpled its clear, dark face.

Flitting lightly from brink to brink,
Followed the garrulous bobolink,
   Rallying loudly with mirthful din,
   The pair who lingered unseen within;
And when from the friendly bridge at last
Into the road beyond they passed,
   Again beside them the tempter went,
   Keeping the thread of his argument:
"*Kiss her! kiss her! chink-a-chee-chee?
I'll not mention it! don't mind me!
   I'll be sentinel; I can see
   All around from this tall birch-tree!*"
But ah! they noted — nor deemed it strange
In his rollicking chorus a trifling change:
   "*Do it! do it!*" with might and main
   Warbled the tell-tale; "*do it again!*"

THE LAST LANDLORD.

YOU who dread the cares and labors
　　Of the tenant's annual quest,
　　You who long for peace and rest,
And the quietest of neighbors,
　　You may find them, if you will,
　　In the city on the hill.

One indulgent landlord leases
　　All the pleasant dwellings there;
　　He has tenants everywhere, —
Every day the throng increases;
　　None may tell their number, yet
　　He has mansions still to let.

Never presses he for payment;
　　Gentlest of all landlords he;
　　And his numerous tenantry
Never lack for food or raiment.
　　Sculptured portal, grassy roof,
　　All alike are trouble-proof.

Of the quiet town's frequenters,
  Never one is ill at ease;
  There are neither locks nor keys,
Yet no robber breaks or enters;
  Not a dweller bolts his door,
  Fearing for his treasure-store.

Never sound of strife or clamor
  Troubles those who dwell therein;
  Never toils distracting din,
Stroke of axe, nor blow of hammer;
  Crimson clover sheds its sweets
  Even in the widest streets.

Never tenant old or younger
  Suffers illness or decline;
  There no suffering children pine;
There comes never want nor hunger;
  Woe and need no longer reign;
  Poverty forgets its pain.

Turmoil and unrest and hurry
  Stay for evermore outside;
  By the hearts which there abide
Wrong, privation, doubt, and worry

Are forgotten quite, or seem
Only like a long-past dream.

Never slander nor detraction
Enters there, and never heard
Is a sharp or cruel word;
No unworthy thought or action,
Purpose or intent of ill,
Knows the city on the hill.

There your mansion never waxes
Out of date, nor needs repairs;
There intrude no sordid cares;
There are neither rent nor taxes;
And no vexed and burdened brain
Reckons either loss or gain.

Wanderers, tired with long endeavor,
You whom, since your being's dawn,
With the stern command " Move on ! "
Ruthless Fate has tracked forever,
Here at last your footsteps stay
With no dread of moving-day !

IF I SHOULD TELL YOU.

IF I should tell you all the bitter woe
    That I have known, — the lonely, toilsome years,
The trampled hopes, the sorrows deep and slow,
    The lacks, the losses, and the hidden tears, —

Your eyes would fill, your tender heart would bleed,
    And you would cry, in sympathetic pain,
" Poor struggling soul, you have been tried indeed;
    Ah, I shall never envy you again!"

But if, instead, I should rehearse to you
    The many blessings which my life has held, —
The happy days, the friends beloved and true,
    The lofty hopes and dreams yet undispelled,

The loves undying, and the peaceful rest, —
    Your ready lips would breathe another strain :
" Thrice favored soul, you have indeed been blest;
    Ah, I shall never pity you again!"

And yet both tales were true ; like all the rest,
  My life has had its bright and gloomy phase;
Ah, happy he who shrines within his breast
  The bright reflection of his sunnier days!

There is no pain without some small relief,
  There is no joy without some pang untold;
The life whose web is warped with darkest grief
  Holds in its woof some threads of tender gold.

And not in vain the thorny way is crossed
  By any earnest soul which, passing through,
Learns only this, — ah, lesson often lost! —
  That other silent souls have suffered too.

So give me still, dear friend, as heretofore
  Smiles for my joy, and tears for my distress,
Since every smile I deem one blessing more,
  And every tear I count one sorrow less.

LAURETTE.

THERE is a touching beauty in the life
   Of a dear daughter, who, while young and fair,
Turns calmly from the beckoning outside world,
Its glittering prospects and fair promises,
And casts her lot beside her mother's hearth,
Becomes a household help and oracle,
And makes a sunshine in her father's house,
To warm and cheer and comfort and sustain
Her honored parents in their waning years,
As did this gentle spirit, — dear Laurette.

She never listened to the stranger's plea,
Nor left the old love for the new, nor sought
A selfish happiness apart from those
Who needed her; but clung where she was born,
Growing more dear and precious year by year,
Until she came to be the household stay,
Her father's staff, her mother's sure right hand,
Trustworthy, diligent, discreet, and wise,

The friend and counsellor of all the rest,
A household saint and helper, — dear Laurette!

The world of strife and show, the heartless world,
Knew nothing of her. She was shrined apart;
She had no share in all its glare and noise;
She lived in shadow, as the violet
Grows up and blooms beneath the orchard tree,
As unassuming, delicate, and shy,
Yet blessing every passer unaware
With the pure beauty of its hidden life,
And when it fades, no other takes its place
Through all the summer's glory. Dear Laurette!

When last she kissed me, with a fond good-by,
She gave me roses. Even while they bloomed
This summer in my garden, she was dead.
Wherefore the thought of her brings back to me
The legend of the sweet Saint Dorothea
Who, ere she died, reached roses from the fields
Of Paradise, and gave them to the friends
She left behind. And so her memory
Shall be like her own roses evermore,
As fragrant and undying. Dear Laurette!

THE STONE-CUTTER.

THERE dwelt in far Japan,
    Long since, a laboring man
Who earned, by hammering stone, his daily food;
    But discontent and dole
    Lay heavy on his soul,
Which craved but riches as the only good.

    And so the gods on high,
    Who sometimes bitterly
Punish a man by granting all his prayers,
    Gave him a mine of gold,
    And lands to have and hold,
And by and by breed feuds among his heirs.

    But soon he, murmuring,
    Desired to be a king;
To reign and rule, — ah, that were perfect bliss!
    He wearied earth and air
    By his incessant prayer,
Until the gods indulged him, even in this.

His courtiers fawned and lied;
And rival powers outside
His realm assailed his peace with fierce debate;
And heaviness and care
Bleached gray his thinning hair,
And made him weary of his royal state.

"Oh, change me to a rock,"
He cried, "that no rude shock
Can stir, nor any storm disturb or shake!"
And lo! he stood ere long
A massive boulder strong,
Which torrents could not move, nor tempests break.

In vain the burning heat
Of fiercest sunshine beat
Upon his head; in vain the storm-wind smote
His rugged sides; in vain
Great rivers, swol'n by rain,
Came roaring from their mountain caves remote.

They moved him not; and he
Rejoiced exceedingly,
And said, "No more for me, O sweet release,

Will there be strife and woe,
And wavering to and fro,
Since I am fixed in an eternal peace!"

But on a summer day
A workman brought that way
A chisel and a hammer, — these alone;
He measured here and there,
And then, with patient care,
Began to cut away the stubborn stone.

"Ah!" said the boulder-king,
"What is this wondrous thing?
This plodding workman smites and conquers me!
He cuts, as suits him best,
Huge blocks from out my breast;
He is more strong than I! would I were he!"

And lo! the powers aloft
Who had so long and oft
Marked his successive follies, soon outgrown,
Again his pleading heard;
He, taken at his word,
Became once more a hammerer of stone!

So, wiser than before,
Desiring nothing more,
Again about his olden toil he went;
Until his ripe old age
He toiled for scanty wage,
And never spake a word of discontent.

WIDOW AND ORPHAN.

SLOWLY the sad night, like a mournful wraith,
   Treads out the daylight, quenching hope and
      faith;
Under the pine-tree we linger, you and I,
While the sky darkens and the winds go by.
Baby, my baby! shake the blossoms from your hair;
Baby, my baby! there be thorns to wear!

Shrouding the shut eyes, keeping out the light,
Cold, cold and heavy, press the sods to-night,
   Freezing the still heart, whence all the warmth is
      gone, —
   Gone, though he said he would love us on and
      on.
Baby, my baby! cold and dark the world has grown;
Baby, my baby! how shall we live alone?

Oh, could we, heaping the cruel earth apart,
Find the dead flowers lying on his heart,

Press the pale lips, which always smiled before,
Kiss the dear hands, which bless us now no more!
Baby, my baby! once he loved us more than all.
Baby, my baby! does he hear our call?

Oh, I could gladly, here beneath the trees,
Wear out these grave-sods with beseeching knees,
  Only to make him hear my voice again,
  Only to tell him all this love and pain.
Baby, my baby! half my love was never said.
Baby, my baby! how shall we wake the dead?

Oh, could we find him by searching every mile
Of earth's broad bosom, — every sea and isle,
  All scorching deserts, every coast and clime, —
  How we should triumph, and conquer space and time!
Baby, my baby! we could walk the wide world through.
Baby, my baby! it were not much to do!

Oh, could we wake him by a thousand years'
Watching and waiting, and weeping bitter tears,
  How should our patience, without loss or lack,
  Wear out the ages, and bring our darling back!

Baby, my baby! Love and Hope and Faith are strong.
Baby, my baby! ages are not long!

But the *forever!* O endless waste of pain!
O thou dear Silent, who answerest not again,
   All the grave's darkness, all death's bitterest strife,
   All cannot equal this lonesome night of life!
Baby, my baby! will the morning ever break?
Baby, my baby! when shall we awake?

EVERY DAY.

O TRIFLING tasks so often done,
 Yet ever to be done anew!
O cares that come with every sun,
 Morn after morn, the long years through!
We shrink beneath their paltry sway, —
The irksome calls of every day.

The restless sense of wasted power,
 The tiresome round of little things,
Are hard to bear, as hour by hour
 Its tedious iteration brings.
Who shall evade, or who delay
The small demands of every day?

The boulder in the torrent's course,
 By tide and tempest lashed in vain,
Obeys the wave-whirled pebble's force,
 And yields its substance, grain by grain;
So crumble strongest lives away
Beneath the wear of every day.

Who finds the lion in his lair,
  Who tracks the tiger for his life,
May wound them ere they are aware,
  Or conquer them in desperate strife,
Yet powerless be to scathe or slay
The vexing gnats of every day.

The steady strain that never stops
  Is mightier than the fiercest shock;
The constant fall of water-drops
  Will groove the adamantine rock;
We feel our noblest powers decay
In feeble wars with every day.

We rise to meet a heavy blow,
  Our souls a sudden bravery fills;
Yet we endure not always so
  The drop-by-drop of little ills;
We still deplore and still obey
The hard behests of every day.

The heart which boldly faces death
  Upon the battlefield, and dares
Cannon and bayonet, faints beneath
  The needle-points of frets and cares;

The stoutest spirits they dismay, —
The tiny stings of every day.

And even saints of holy fame,
    Whose souls by faith have overcome,
Who wore, amid the cruel flame,
    The molten crown of martyrdom,
Bore not without complaint alway
The petty pains of every day.

Ah! more than martyr's aureole,
    And more than hero's heart of fire,
We need the humble strength of soul
    Which daily toils and ills require.
Sweet patience, fill our souls, we pray,
With added grace for every day!

A SUMMER MELODY.

AMID the keys of the organ,
  Lies hidden a tender tune,
Whose tremulous chords interpret
  The soul of a night in June,
Ere Jupiter's steady splendor
  Is dimmed by the late full moon.

It seems like an eve in summer,
  When the stars are near and bright;
It keeps the breath of the jasmine
  That sweetens the moist, still night,
But loses its mystical fragrance
  In the chill of morning light.

It haunts me, awake and dreaming,
  That soft, mysterious air;
It will not come at my bidding,
  Yet follows me everywhere,
Tender with passionate longing,
  And wild with a vague despair.

Like a possible joy ungathered
   In the blinded days of old ;
Like a hope that, long unblossomed,
   Might yet to the light unfold,
If fortune were not so cruel,
   If the world were not so cold.

How softly they gather about me,
   The shadows and scents of June,
The steady light of a planet,
   The dawn of the rising moon,
Born of remembered music, —
   That tender and wistful tune !

Eluding my voice and fingers,
   It rings in my dreaming brain,
Now jubilant as in triumph,
   Now wailing in wordless pain.
Alas, for a hand to waken
   Its magical notes again !

THE LILAC-TREE.

CHANT-ROYAL.

BECAUSE the rose and lily have been sung
    By every bard that ever tuned a lyre,
And daisies, may, and pansies have been flung
On every altar, touched or not with fire;
Because the jessamine's faint stars of white
Are always making sweet the summer night,
Whenever lovers sing a roundelay;
And the shy violet, this many a day,
Has been despoiled of all her modesty
By being praised in every poet's lay, —
I sing the beauty of the lilac-tree!

The patient ivy-vine has crept and clung
In every poem, till it can but tire;
The woodbine wandered in and out among
The daffodils and myrtle and sweet-brier,
In all the songs since earliest poet's flight,
Whether of laurelled bard, or neophyte;
And we, grown weary of the hackneyed way,

Crave something that has not been twined with bay,
And made a byword in all minstrelsy;
Wherefore, in all sincerity, I say
I sing the glory of the lilac-tree.

Because we loved it so when we were young,
And knew nor worldly dolor nor desire;
Its heart-shaped leaves in wilting wreaths we strung,
Nor wept to see them wither and expire;
Beneath its roof of flickering shade and light
We talked of fairies, beautiful and bright,
And spread our banquet-board as children may,
A Barmecidal feast, which only they
Whose eyes were clear with youth could ever see:
Because of those sweet days of happy play,
I sing thy praises, kindly lilac-tree!

How fair it stood, with purple tassels hung,
Their hue more tender than the tint of Tyre!
How musical amid their fragrance rung
The bee's bassoon, key-note of spring's glad choir!
O languorous lilac! still in time's despite
I see thy plumy branches all alight
With new-born butterflies, which loved to stay
And bask and banquet in the temperate ray

Of spring-time, ere the torrid heats should be;
For these dear memories, though the world grow
    gray,
I sing thy sweetness, lovely lilac-tree!

Oh for a sweeter voice, a readier tongue,
A lighter touch upon the tuneful wire!
No tree more beautiful has ever sprung
Since first a green leaf grew from earthly mire.
Thou shrinkest from the warm and withering blight
Of human touch; unlike the favorite
Of poets, rose or lily, thou alway
Refusest to be sold for sordid pay;
The street and market-place are death to thee:
Because thou wilt not live the spoiler's prey,
I sing thy praises, sensitive lilac-tree!

Oh, touch my forehead with thy purple spray!
Bid me not worship thee, lest I obey.
The Persian's flower-adoring shocks not me;
So, lovingly, though all the world say nay,
I sing my fealty to the lilac-tree!

THE SWEETEST SLEEP.

POOR heart, worn out with aching,
    With troubled dreaming and with joyless waking,
        How sweet and well-attended
Shall be thy rest, when all thy toils are ended!

    Thy tired head pillowed purely
In virgin earth, there shalt thou sleep securely;
        Not one shall dare molest thee,
Of all the cruel ills which have oppressed thee.

    Those whom thy love has cherished
May weep for thee, and mourn that thou hast perished;
        But grass will grow about thee,
And all the world go on the same without thee.

    Perhaps, for one brief summer,
The birds will fly before some lonely comer
        Who used to prize and love thee,
And stays to strew fresh flowers and tears above thee.

But love grows weary, sighing
To silent hearts which utter no replying;
　　Awhile he will regret thee,
Then wipe his eyes, and sigh, and so forget thee.

　　The butterfly, alighted
Upon thy peaceful bosom, unaffrighted,
　　Shall sip the blooms above thee,
And spread and shut his wings, unmindful of thee.

　　The cuckoo, for thy hearing,
Shall pour his tender monotone unfearing;
　　The whippoorwill bewail thee,
With tender constancy that shall not fail thee.

　　The brook, from reedy cover,
Shall tell the story of thy lifetime over
　　To the dim shades which throng thee,
Nor once in all the sweet recital wrong thee.

　　Shy wood-birds, which love only
The haunts which men have left untracked and
　　　　lonely,
　　Upon the sods which hide thee
Shall drink the dew, and sit and sing beside thee.

At eve, the clear-voiced thrushes
Shall make the sweet air throb with music-gushes,
   Yet wake no thrill within thee,
Nor from thy deep undreaming slumber win thee.

The timid rabbit, stopping,
With ears alert, to hear the acorns dropping,
   Shall pass unscared, and leave thee,
And turn with quick bright eyes, yet not perceive thee.

The squirrel, at his pleasure
Frisking, shall fill his cheeks with winter treasure,
   And with no cause to fear thee,
Shell his ripe nuts, and dig his storehouse near thee.

The pine that guards thy sleeping,
Shall hold thy memory in fragrant keeping,
   With balsam-tears deplore thee,
And build with cones an odorous altar o'er thee.

And when the autumn passes,
And fades thy coverlet of plumy grasses,
   Nature shall not neglect thee,
But send her whitest angels to protect thee.

Then, burdened heart, with patience
Bear thou thy load of trials and temptations,
For sweet and well-attended
Shall be thy sleep, when all thy toils are ended!

HER LIFE LONG.

ONCE, long ago, in spring's most gracious weather,
　　A newly wedded pair, with hearts at rest,
　　Watched while a bluebird wove into its nest
A shred, a twig, a straw, a downy feather, —
　　Laughing like two glad children; they were blest
Wholly, in that they loved, and were together,
　　And May and life and hope were at their best.

Love's brightest garlands, fair and freshly braided,
　　About her way their richest fragrance threw,
　　Yet with a woman's prescient fear she knew
How men, grown tired of faces worn and shaded,
　　Seek otherwhere youth's morning bloom and dew;
"Ah, love!" she cried, "when I am old and faded,
　　Say, will you love me still, and still be true?"

In what most eager haste of fond replying
　　He soothed her doubt, and hushed her tender fears
With all the vows most sweet to woman's ears,

Soft foolish names, and happiest prophesying!
   (Yet he had been — so time at lovers jeers —
When, ten long lustrums after, he lay dying,
   Another's mate for more than two-score years!)

By those sweet eyes, upraised in wistful query
   To him so dearly loved, so lately wed,
Woman's most bitter tears were never shed;
She never mourned for love grown false or weary,
   Or sat in dust, with ashes on her head,
In age and solitude, forgotten, dreary, —
   For ere her youth had faded, she was dead.

Ah, happy she, to die with faith unblighted,
   Before life's dawn had lost its rose-and-gold,
   Or the one trusted heart grown hard and cold!
Not hers the anguish of a true soul slighted,
   Humbled and rent for things of baser mould;
Happy indeed is she, who, early plighted,
   Finds youth means love — and dies ere she grows
      old!

FLOWERS IN RAIN.

STEADY and small, the summer rain
    Drops freshness, all the long day through,
The lilac-tree takes heart again,
    And trims her purple plumes anew;

The opulent viburnum's robes
    Trail, heavy-weighted by the shower;
While slowly all its light-green globes
    Whiten to snowballs hour by hour.

Sweet incense-breaths of gratitude
    Betray the valley-lily meek;
And from the shade in cheerful mood
    The pansy lifts its velvet cheek.

Yet some of June's fair pensioners
    Love not this gray and weeping sky;
The chestnut silently demurs,
    And drops its blossoms patiently;

The lush red peony, yesterday
  Lighting the garden's wonder-land,
Lies low along the gravelled way,
  Its burning forehead in the sand;

The dandelions shrink and close,
  Loving the sun and lacking him,
Dishevelled with their watery woes,
  And all their golden disks grown dim.

SOME DAY.

YOU smooth the tangles from my hair,
    With gentle touch and tenderest care,
    And count the years ere you shall mark
    Bright silver threads among the dark,
Smiling, the while, to hear me say,
" You 'll think of this again, some day,
            Some day ! "

I do not scorn the power of time,
Nor count on years of fadeless prime;
    But no white gleams will ever shine
    Among these heavy locks of mine.
Ah, laugh as gaily as you may,
You 'll think of this again, some day,
            Some day!

Some day I shall not feel, as now,
Your soft hand move about my brow;
    I shall not slight your light commands,
    And draw my tresses through your hands;

I shall be silent, and obey;
And you — you will not laugh, that day, —
          Some day!

I know how long your loving hands
Will linger with these glossy bands,
   When you shall weave my latest crown
   Of their thick masses, long and brown;
But you will see no touch of gray
Adown their shining length, that day, —
          Some day!

And while your tears are falling hot
Upon the lips which answer not,
   You 'll take from these one treasured tress
   And leave the rest to silentness,
Remembering that I used to say,
"You 'll think of this again some day, —
          Some day!"

COULD SUMMER LAST FOREVER.

FAINT bronzy hints of autumn brown
    Proclaim the chilly comer;
The first red leaf comes floating down,
    A sign of vanished summer.
Alas! how lately did the earth
    In spring's fair garments robe her,
And June laugh out for very mirth —
    And now here comes October!
A breath of autumn chills the day,
    A faint prophetic shiver;
Why cannot sunshine always stay,
    And summer last forever?

On hillside, field, and meadow wide
    Appear the changing tinges;
The golden-rod on every side
    Shakes out its shining fringes;
The purple disks of asters rise
    In all the wayside places;
The frost, beneath night's still, clear skies,
    Its dainty broidery traces;

Alas! but now the willows dropped
   Their catkins in the river.
Why could not time's swift wheels be stopped,
   And summer last forever?

It was but now the bluebird sang
   In leafless garden alleys,
And April smiled, and new grass sprang
   In all the sheltered valleys.
It was but now the bees were lost
   In bloomy wastes and mazes,
And, foam-like, on green billows tossed
   White crests of ox-eye daisies.
Ah, for some realm where blossom-friends
   Would change and perish never,
Some clime where flower-time never ends,
   And summer lasts forever!

But now the early flowers looked up,
   The fields and pastures over, —
Shy innocence, bold buttercup,
   And white and crimson clover;
The violet peeped through sodden leaves,
   In sunny, snow-soaked hollows;

And maples bloomed, and country eaves
    Were all a-chirp with swallows.
The nested broods have come and gone;
    With dread the maples quiver;
Oh, could the sun shine on and on,
    And summer last forever!

The warblers all are fled or mute;
    The gray skies frown and lower;
The orchard trees have lost their fruit;
    The shorn fields have no flower.
The evening cricket chirps, alas,
    His shrill foreboding warning,
And dew-bright webs festoon the grass
    In roadside fields at morning.
All things foretell how soon delight
    And our pale world must sever.
Ah, could the sky be always bright,
    And summer last forever!

Ah, life would be supremely blest
    If youth were not so fleeting,
If June would come at our behest,
    Or stay for our entreating;

But frost and bloom, and youth and age
　Must rule the world together,
And calendars still keep a page
　For months of winter weather.
But when relinquished evermore
　Is life's intent endeavor,
Shall we not find a fairer shore
　Where summer lasts forever?

UNWEDDED.

O THOU beloved, who shouldst have been mine
   own,
Serenely beautiful and wise and strong,
Consoler whom my life has never known,
   How have I missed thee, seeking thee alone
      All my life long?

Somewhere upon the wide and misty track
   I strayed behind, or did not wait for thee,
And so must always mourn my bitter lack,
   Since on this weary road we go not back,
      Ah, woe is me!

Often, with sorely burdened heart and mind,
   When there were none to aid or understand,
How have I groped, with tears, alone and blind,
   In the thick darkness, longing but to find
      Thy helpful hand!

For I believed that Love is doubly armed
   Against all foes, and with unshaken breath
Could pass through pain and suffering unalarmed,
   Could take up poisonous things yet not be harmed,
      And dare even death.

" And how shall Love, immortal and sublime,"
   I said, " be hindered of its best estate
By any petty chance of space or time?"
   Alas, my life has lost its freshest prime,
      And still I wait.

How beautiful our mingled lives had been
   Had we but found each other in our youth!
The world had grown, despite its stain and sin,
   Sweeter because we two had lived therein
      Our utter truth.

Then all the myriad ills which Fate contrives
   Wherewith to fret men's hearts, to us had been
But motes along the sunshine of our lives;
   Naught could have harmed us, since the true soul thrives
      By discipline.

Then this unending toil and ceaseless toss
  Had never marred my life; the hindering load
Of worldly circumstance, of gain or loss,
  Had seemed to us but cobwebs, stretched across
    Our upward road.

Where art thou, love? Far as the farthest pole,
  Hast thou, too, vaguely dreamed of what should
    be?
Or, mated early with some feebler soul,
  Hast struggled with thy bonds in grief and dole,
    Longing for me?

I had been more than all the world to thee,
  So proudly tender, so entirely true,
So wise and tireless in my ministry,
  More dear than any other soul could be,
    All my life through.

Alas! the sun's last glimmering has kissed
  The highest mountain-tops to gold; and now
The crimson west has changed to amethyst,
  And all the vale is dim with chilly mist,
    But where art thou?

Too late! too late! the darkness gathereth,
  And the night falleth, pitiless and dumb.
I cannot reach thee with this hopeless breath;
  But when I walk the other side of death,
    Wilt thou not come?

IN THE FIELDS.

ONCE more amid your pleasant scenes, New England fields and woods,
Your shining streams and sunny farms and shady solitudes,
Your pastures with their grazing herds, content and sleek and mute,
Your fair long rows of orchard trees, adroop with rosy fruit.

I pluck the brilliant golden-rod and asters at my feet;
I climb the vine-draped boulder, and pull the bittersweet;
I thread the deepest brookside dells to find the gentian blue,
And in sweet Nature's youth and joy, am young and joyful too.

O wood-paths, wild wood-paths, in days remembered well,
I walked unsnared amid your toils, nor ever tripped nor fell;
O'er tangled stems and twisted roots I bounded lightly then,
Sure-footed as the antelope in wildest mountain glen.

Alas, alas! my foot has lost the cunning of old days;
I stumble in the briery paths; I shun the rocky ways;
The brambles tear my careless hair, and try to hold me back;
The thorn-boughs stab me as I pass, then close and hide my track.

O blackbird, glad blackbird, that warbles all the day,
Deep in the laden orchards, the old familiar lay,
When last I strolled as now among the stubble of the wheat,
You scarcely ceased your whistling at the rustle of my feet;

You scarcely flew before me, as I came more near
and near,
But sat unscared, and sang as if for me alone to
hear;
While now you hear my greeting voice with wonder
and affright,
With sudden sidelong glances, and swift suspicious
flight.

O squirrel in the oak-tree, where are your acorns
stored?
I used to find your hiding-place, and wonder at your
hoard;
We were fast friends and playmates then; oh,
wherefore shun me now,
And chatter small defiance from the tall tree's top-
most bough?

O Nature, mother Nature, with your soul so strong
and true,
What fate has snapped the tender bond that kept
me close to you, —
The quick, electric sympathy alive to thrill and
tone,
Which made your thousand varying moods seem
echoes of my own?

True, I have wandered far away from all I prized
in youth;
But I have loved the forest still, with strong un-
swerving truth,
Amid the city's noise have heard the far-off song of
streams,
And rambled all the well-known woods and hill-
sides in my dreams.

Oh, take me to your heart again, and give to me once
more
The loving, pure, believing soul I had in days of
yore!
Shut all the tiresome world away, protect me and
defend,
And be, as in my happier youth, my mother and my
friend!

BEFORE DARK.

COLD, untender eyes, calm and steady,
   Lips with chill replies always ready,
  Wear your mask, forsooth; but a while hence
  Time shall wring the truth from your silence;
You will clasp the mound piled above me,
Owning then, tear-drowned, that you love me!

You will seek me yet, undissembling,
With your proud eyes wet, and lips trembling,
  And forbearing so to misdoubt me,
  Make white roses blow all about me;
Shall I feel them sigh sweet above me?
Tell me, ere I die, that you love me!

When I turn my face from all weeping,
You will haunt the place of my sleeping,
  And, no longer fain then to grieve me,
  Wail remorseful pain. Ah, believe me!
Then your bitterest cry cannot move me.
Tell me, ere I die, that you love me!

Lips forever still will not bless you;
Cold hands will not thrill to caress you;
   Dead ears will not list vow or pleading;
   Eyes too seldom kissed sleep unheeding;
Prayers cannot again lift their lashes;
Love entreats in vain dust and ashes!

A STRATFORD WILD-ROSE.

THIS wild-rose, plucked by Avon's side,
   Is not a whit more sweet or fair
Than those which brighten summer-tide
   In dear New England's air;

But this is of a noble line
   Which held, in yonder century,
A privilege, by right divine,
   That now no gold could buy;

A privilege of rarer fame
   Than any prince of royal blood,
Or any king on earth can claim;
   So is this half-blown bud

Ennobled, not by wealth or wars,
   But by the truth that it may trace
Its lineage back to ancestors
   Who looked on Shakspeare's face.

For oft by Avon's pleasant stream,
   In youth's unspoiled light-heartedness,
Did he, the marvellous, rove and dream,
   And pluck a rose like this.

They saw — those eyes which never missed
   The smallest flower, the humblest leaf —
These golden anthers, dewdrop-kissed,
   Or robbed by wingèd thief.

Such thorns dared wound him with their sting,
   Such leaves within his warm hand curled,
Nor recognized the uncrowned king
   Whose realm was all the world.

Such petals fell about his feet,
   And clung upon them, wet with dew;
They breathed the selfsame airy sweet,
   And wore the selfsame hue.

Wild-roses grow by Avon's side
   To-day, as then they used to grow,
When Shakspeare watched its rippling tide,
   Three hundred years ago.

And softly still the hallowed stream,
  Whose murmur, as he roved along,
Commingled with his boyish dream,
  Repeats the selfsame song;

While he, whose praise the ages sound,
  Who gave its wave a deathless name,
And made his birthplace sacred ground,
  Is only dust — and fame.

Thus do earth's mightiest fade and cease;
  Even the poor dust within their tombs
Is lost, as centuries increase;
  But still the wild-rose blooms.

FAITHFUL UNTO DEATH.

IN the wise books of ancient lore we find,
"Full many meet the gods, but few salute
them."
The sages knew that men are deaf and blind;
And who in modern days shall dare dispute
them?

But I, O precious friend of many years,
In the first moment of our casual meeting,
I knew the visitant from loftier spheres;
I recognized the god, and gave him greeting.

Thank Heaven for that! I knew you at a glance;
I did not need to test or try or doubt you;
I read your birthright in your countenance;
I saw the mystic halo shine about you.

What though some eyes were blind, and could not
see
The light divine, nor note the crowning splendor?
It was enough so true and great to be
To those you loved,— so kindly, wise, and tender.

Through all the years, whatever grief befell
  My life, whatever cruel pain assailed me,
Your heart has been my sheltering citadel,
  Your tender, helpful love has never failed me.

A faithful and unfailing comradeship,
  My stronghold in this world of evanescence,
Consoling words, kind eyes, and smiling lip, —
  I found them all in your most gracious presence.

Had all the breathing world conspired to prove
  That you could wrong me, slight me, or deceive me,
Not all the world had made me doubt your love,
  Or wrong your utter truth. Dear ghost, believe me!

O friend most dear! my way is full of fears;
  To-day is dreary, and I dread to-morrow.
How shall I bear the bleak and bitter years
  Which I must meet in loneliness and sorrow?

How can I bear what I could not have borne
  Even when my heart was happier and younger, —
The memories which only make me mourn,
  The solitude, the spirit's thirst and hunger?

Through these remaining days of mortal breath
   I can but weep you, miss you, and regret you,
Knowing no solace but that after death
   My soul must either find you — or forget you!

TWO LIVES.

WHEN last the earth was green
    Under the summer's sheen,
And shrub and weed were breaking into flower,
    One of my lilies sweet
    Drooped in the pitiless heat,
And fainted and grew feebler, hour by hour.

    Its leaves drooped sadly down,
    And withered, dry and brown;
Its stems were shrivelled, even in early June.
    Alas, untimely doomed,
    With all its buds unbloomed!
"Ah, cruel Death," I said, "to come so soon!"

    Yet of the woes which fate
    Holds for us, soon or late,
Bringing to each his load for soul and brain,
    Not theirs the dreariest doom
    Who die before their bloom,
And lose life's joys, while they escape its pain.

In February's air
One of my rose-trees fair
Pushed its red shoots, as if the spring were here;
Fresh leaves unrolled and grew;
Buds drank the chilly dew,
And dared to dream their blossom-time was near.

But ere the eldest one
Had opened to the sun,
Across the garden fell a bitter frost;
The rose-tree in its pride,
Was stricken that it died,
With all its tender promise blighted, lost.

And when the spring's slow grace
Came back and blessed the place,
The rose no longer sprouted by the gate.
In vain the breeze beguiled;
In vain the sunlight smiled.
"Ah, cruel Love," I said, "to come so late!"

Alas! in life's long list
Of blessings lost or missed,
Of wrong, and early blight, and slighted trust,
Theirs is the saddest fate
To whom love comes too late,
And showers with useless tears their lifeless dust!

O CRICKET, HUSH!

O CRICKET, hush your boding song!
  I know the truth it makes so plain;
You say that autumn dies ere long,
And soon the winter's wrath and wrong
  Will chill the pallid world again.

O mournful winds of midnight, cease
  To breathe your low, prophetic sigh;
Too clearly for my spirit's peace
I see the mellow days decrease,
  And feel December drawing nigh.

Fall silently, October rain,
  Nor take that wailing undertone,
Nor beat so loudly on the pane
The sad, monotonous refrain
  Which tells me summer-time has flown.

Be charier of your golden days,
    O goldenest month of all the throng!
Oh, pour less lavishly your rays!
Hoard carefully your purple haze,
    So haply it may last more long!

Spendthrift October, art thou wise,
    Who wastest, in thy plenteous prime,
More beauty on the earth and skies,
More hue and glow, than would suffice
    To brighten all the winter-time?

Yes, better autumn all delight,
    And then a winter all unblest,
Than months of mingled dark and bright,
Of faded tints and pallid light,
    Imperfect dreams and broken rest.

Ah, better if our life could know
    One wholly happy, perfect year,
One time of cloudless joy and glow,
And then its days of rayless woe,
    Than this commingled hope and fear;

This doubt and dread which naught consoles,
  Which mark our brows ere manhood's prime ;
The dread uncertainty that rolls
Like chariot-wheels across our souls,
  And makes us old before our time.

So pour your light, October skies!
  O fairest skies which ever are !
Put on, O earth, your bravest dyes,
And smile, although the cricket cries,
  And winter threatens from afar!

TEARS.

TEARS on a blooming cheek, — dew on a rose!
   Who would not kiss them, and charm them away?
Called to soft eyes by the briefest of woes,
   Showers from the blue of a morning in May.
Tears on a blooming cheek, — dew on a rose!
   Rainbowed with smiles are the tears of the young;
Light is the sorrow that maidenhood knows;
   Sweet is the solace by flattery sung.
      Beauty need never seek
      Vainly for Love to speak;
Tears on a blooming cheek, — dew on a rose!

Tears on a faded cheek, — rain on a tomb!
   Yet who deplores them or wipes them away?
Wrung from a soul that has wandered in gloom,
   Homeless and hopeless, for many a day;

Tears on a faded cheek, — rain on a tomb!
 Bitter, alas, are the tears of the old,
Staining a face long forsaken of bloom;
 Love has forgotten the story he told;
  Faith has grown cold and weak;
  Life's road is lone and bleak;
Tears on a faded cheek, — rain on a tomb!

OVER SEA.

WE two were lovers; and side by side,
    One rare and beautiful summer-tide,
Like children roaming in light and dew.
Broad fields and woodlands and meadows through,
Their faces radiant with morning gleams,
We sought the scenes of our early dreams.
    We crossed the waste of the broad blue deep,
    Saw sunbeams gild it, or fierce winds sweep;
But all its changes were fair to me,
For calm and tempest were sweet with thee.

By English hedges we took our way,
And watched the bloom of the fragrant may;
    We paused and listened, with lifted eyes,
    The lark translated in morning skies;
We sipped, at close of the dreamy day,
The fruity nectar of Epernay;
    We threaded happily, hand in hand,
    The blossomy valleys of Switzerland,
And drank the milk of the goats which climb
The high Alp-pastures in summer-time.

We plucked the heath of the Apennines,
And pulled the clusters of Tuscan vines;
   We dipped our hands in the azure sea
   That kisses the border of Italy;
We walked in the haunted ways of Rome;
We bathed our foreheads in Trevi's foam;
   We watched the flow of the storied Rhine,
   And saw in moonlight the Arno shine;
And all fair places, I could but see,
Owed half their wonderful charm to thee.

But sweeter farings were yet to be, —
We were to cross the Indian sea;
   To breathe, enchanted, the rich perfume
   Where Persia's gardens of roses bloom;
To hear the bulbul at shut of night
Fill all the shadows with rare delight;
   To rest in the shade of the Pyramids;
   To see the lotus unclose its lids;
And all the marvellous realms that be,
All were to be mine own, — with thee!

Alas for all that we dreamed and planned!
No more thy careful and loving hand
   Will smooth the paths for my happy feet,
   As in that summer so brief and sweet.

I shall not walk in the pleasant ways
Of which we talked in the dear bright days;
    The paths which wait me lie rough and steep
    Across bleak hillsides, through shadows deep, —
Paths sadder than any my feet have known,
Because, alas! I must walk alone.

The spring will shine on the distant shore
So fondly pictured in days of yore;
    Fair ships will sail on the Indian sea,
    With glad hearts freighted; but not for me
Will Persia's love-songs be softly sung,
Or Stamboul's roses in chaplets strung;
    And not for me will the sweet airs blow
    Through odorous groves where the plantains grow,
And the palm's fair fruit, and the banyan-tree;
I lost them all, love, in losing thee!

For since that summer, a grievous change
Has made my future all dark and strange;
    Thy grave is under a northern sky
    Where tempests frown, and the winds go by;
Thy rest is watched by the northern star;
And kneeling by thee, I hear afar

The surf's faint roar and the sea-bird's call;
The trees stand bare, by the frosty wall;
The sleet slants sharply and bitterly,
And all is winter, away from thee.

I shall not rove where the tamarinds grow,
And breaths of spice from the gardens flow;
  The lovely places we should have known
  Would be but anguish to me, alone;
The orange-flowers and roses rare
Would fade and wither adown my hair;
  The bulbul's love-notes, from thee apart,
  Would stab like daggers, and pierce my heart;
The far fair tropics are not for me,
For all my summer is gone with thee!

SOME HEARTS GO HUNGERING.

SOME hearts go hungering through the world,
    And never find the love they seek;
Some lips with pride or scorn are curled
    To hide the pain they may not speak.
The eye may flash, the mouth may smile,
    The voice in gladdest music thrill,
And yet beneath them all the while
    The hungry heart be pining still.

These know their doom, and walk their way
    With level steps and steadfast eyes,
Nor strive with Fate, nor weep, nor pray;
    While others, not so sadly wise,
Are mocked by phantoms evermore,
    And lured by seemings of delight
Fair to the eye, but at the core
    Holding but bitter dust and blight.

I see them gaze from wistful eyes;
    I mark their sign in fading cheeks;
I hear them breathe in smothered sighs,
    And note the grief that never speaks.

For them no might redresses wrong,
   No eye with pity is impearled.
O misconstrued and suffering long,
   O hearts that hunger through the world!

For you does life's dull desert hold
   No fountained shade, no date-grove fair,
No gush of waters clear and cold,
   But sandy reaches, wide and bare;
The foot may fail, the soul may faint,
   And weigh to earth the weary frame;
But still ye make no weak complaint,
   And speak no word of grief or blame.

O eager eyes which gaze afar!
   O arms which clasp the empty air!
Not all unmarked your sorrows are,
   Not all unpitied your despair.
Smile, patient lips so proudly dumb,
   When life's frail tent at last is furled,
Your glorious recompense shall come,
   O hearts that hunger through the world!

LATE OCTOBER.

THE cruel frost has left no bloom alive,
  But playful Nature seems to try how fair
    Her skill can make the wood
    Without the help of flowers.

And so she pranks the leaves with hues as bright
As any that the summer blossoms wore;
    The sumac's robes are dyed
    With brilliant red and gold,

The maple glows with every varying tint
Of scarlet, luminous yellow, unchanged green,
    And myriad shadings, born
    Of all these mingled hues.

The regal oak puts on its bravest dress,
Purple and crimson; while the humbler beech,
    In pallid russet, dreads
    The next dishevelling breeze.

Timid and terrified, the poplar stands,
Shivering in thinnest yellow, though the leaves
    Of other trees are still,
    And all the winds at rest.

The sunshine, melting through the gorgeous roof,
Fills all the wood with strange, unwonted light,
    And makes the atmosphere
    A bath of liquid gold,

Wherein all turbulent thoughts, discordant sounds,
And dissonant voices seem dissolved away
    Into a perfect peace,
    A truce from all the world.

How silent! there is not a sound to break
The utter quiet of the autumn noon,
    Save when an acorn drops
    Upon the crisp dead leaves,

Or suddenly a prickly chestnut-burr,
Scorning to wait for the compelling wind,
    Falls, and rebounds again,
    Scattering its treasures wide.

A squirrel, frisking in the thinning boughs,
Flings down a half-shelled nut before my feet,
    And chattering noisily,
    Disputes the intruder's right,

Or, in the shadow of his plumy tail,
Stands motionless, and silent as a leaf,
    Peering with wild bright eyes,
    Curious, yet half afraid,

Then, swift and nimble, scampers up aloft,
Surefooted sailor of the sea of leaves,
    Fearless of dizzy heights
    And heaving depths below.

Hark! from afar a faint, unanswered call!
The lonesome cry of some belated bird,
    Left by his emigrant tribe
    To meet the frost alone;

And like a dirge for all the insect lives
Which made the wood of late so voluble,
    The last faint katydid
    Rasps feebly in the fern.

Yonder a leaf-brown rabbit from the brake
Leaps, and is lost amid his kindred hues;
    The sudden rustle dies;
    And all is still again.

"IN EVERY PORT."

THE captain follows the sea no more,
  But spends the eve of his days on shore;
And when about him an eager band
Beg for a tale of the sea or land,
The gentlest among them plead and coax
For the sad, strange story of Jasper Oakes.

" The ship was ready, the cargo stored,
The wind was willing, the crew on board;
And we sailed away from the English shore
For fair Manhattan, our home, once more;
But halfway over, there came a blow
That threatened to sink us fathoms low.

" The mate I had shipped on the trip before
Was the bravest fellow on wave or shore, —
A thorough seaman, alert and wise,
And wondrous handsome, with fearless eyes,
A swift sure foot, and a steady hand;
A right good comrade, on sea or land.

"A jib swung loose in the roaring gale;
'Up,' I shouted, ' and furl the sail!'
Before another could make reply,
The mate sprang forward and cried, 'Ay, ay!
I am the oldest sailor here!'
'Stay!' I screamed in his heedless ear;

"' Fasten a rope's end round you, then,
Even sailors are only men;
A dip of the boom will break your hold.'
'No!' he shouted, unwisely bold,
' Never a cowardly rope for me;
Tether a squirrel to climb a tree!'

"The laboring vessel, with creak and strain,
Struggled and groaned like a thing in pain;
But Oakes, the bravest of all my men,
Never stood on the deck again.
He was torn from his hold by the mad waves' might,
And the wild sea swallowed him out of sight.

"My gallant shipmate! I missed him sore,
And grieved as I seldom grieved before,
Yet, in my brooding, was glad to know
What he had told me a time ago:

'I 've not a tie in the world,' said he;
'A ship is my sweetheart, my home the sea.

"'And if I choke in the bitter brine,
Nobody's venture goes down but mine!'
So I rejoiced that no hearth was dim,
No fond heart broken, because of him;
That no sad woman would pine and wait,
Or come and ask for the missing mate.

"Past the Narrows and up the bay,
Home we came on a bright March day,
Glad of our harbor; and almost ere
The vessel touched at the well-known pier,
Lightly over the side there came
A slip of a girl, who called my name.

"She had a face like an early rose,
And the smile of a child, who hardly knows
What the burden of living means, —
Scarcely out of her happy teens;
'And who,' I asked, 'do you chance to be?
And what, my girl, do you want with me?'

"'Only your mate,' with a smile more sweet;
'Your mate, my husband, I came to meet —

I could not wait, sir, a moment more;
I could not stay till he came on shore.
I hope,' — she paused, and her face grew dim, —
'I hope no evil has chanced to him?'

"Stunned for a moment, I scarcely knew
Whether my eyes and ears were true;
Yet there she stood, in her hopeful youth,
Her whole face earnest with love and truth,
Eager and anxious, with lips apart,
Waiting for news that would break her heart!

"'Out on the jib-boom, in a gale,
He went in the darkness, to furl a sail;
The vessel struggled and plunged and tossed;
The ropes were icy — and he was lost.'
Bitter and cruel words, I knew;
But what could a clumsy sailor do?

"Out of her face, in an instant white,
Vanished the glow, like a blown-out light,
The smile of joy, and the beaming hope;
And down she dropped on a coil of rope,
Wringing her hands with moans of woe,
Like one struck blind by a sudden blow.

"The pitying sailors kindly bore
The poor girl-widow back on shore,
And the mate's sea-chest, and the little hoard
Of foreign trinkets he had on board;
But her poor pale face, with its grief and fright,
Haunted my dreams for many a night.

" With April's sunshine and breezes cool,
We bowled back blithely to Liverpool;
And when, at the close of a cloudy day,
In front of its dingy wharves we lay,
Crossing the deck, I chanced to see
A fair-faced woman, who asked for me.

" No fresh young girl, with a rosy face,
But a woman, wearing a matron's grace,
In whose soft eyes, as they questioned mine,
I saw the look of a mother shine;
And closely grasping her garment's fold,
Was a three years' baby, with hair like gold.

" With a chill that smote like a sudden blast,
I thought of the woman who stood there last,
Sinking under her great despair;
And my glance grew into a startled stare,

As the boy came forward, and gazed at me
With the eyes of the man I had lost at sea.

"'Where is Oakes?' asked a voice of doubt,
'Who sailed with you on your voyage out?
I am his wife; have I come too late?
Has he gone on shore? Do you hesitate?
Speak to me! tell me! Ah, I see
You are keeping some terrible truth from me!'

"Staggered, breathless, in dazed surprise
Under the spell of those well-known eyes, —
Eyes which silenced my struggling doubt, —
"'Lost'— I gasped —'on the passage out —
Lost from the jib-boom — furling sail —
Overboard — in a heavy gale.'"

Thus, as the captain quaffs and smokes,
He tells the story of Jasper Oakes.

A HYACINTH.

A HYACINTH'S lovely completeness
   Unfolds to the chilly spring day,
A marvel of color and sweetness.
   O tender-faced step-child of May,
Ere scarcely the winter is over,
   You come with consoling amends;
The wild fickle wind is your lover,
   And the cloud and the cold are your friends!

The wild fickle wind is your lover;
   He searches through snowflakes and gloom
Your winter retreat to discover,
   And kisses your cheek into bloom;
He charms you with tenderest praising,
   Till, weary of fragrance and you,
He finds where the tulips are blazing,
   And whispers his love-tale anew.

Do we love you because you are lonely?
   And is it, sweet helper, the truth,
That freshness and novelty only
   Made all the lost glamour of youth?

Or are joys really dearest and fleetest,
  Which spring's doubtful dawning has nursed?
Is life's early dream, then, its sweetest?
  Is there never a love like the first?

Ah, blest, that your season of blooming
  Has come ere the wet earth is warm, —
Ere yet the bold beetle comes booming
  To carry your sweetness by storm;
Ere yet on the billowy breezes,
  Unchallenged, unhindered, and free
To rob and despoil as he pleases,
  Comes sailing the freebooter bee.

The sluggard! for yet he reposes
  Enshrined amid nectar-filled cells;
His dreams are of jasmine and roses,
  But never of hyacinth-bells.
No vision of you ever crosses
  His sleep in his honeyed estate.
Ah, well if we guess not the losses
  Which come of our waking too late!

When breezes grow gentle and mellow,
  Narcissus and daffodils vain
Will flutter in white and in yellow
  And call him to conquest again;

But woe to the bloom where he settles,
   Most rude and remorseless of thieves ;
No shower can wash from its petals
   The track which his violence leaves.

He takes without promise or payment,
   And little he pities or knows
The stain on the lily's white raiment,
   Or the sigh of the heartbroken rose.
You will die ere that harshest of masters
   Can work you his flattering wrong;
It is well to perceive what disasters
   Might come of our living too long!

Yet stay till these petulant showers
   Have finished their mission of grace,
And brought the less beautiful flowers
   To claim — though they fill not — your place ;
Till spring's chilly twilight is over,
   And April's uncertainty ends ;
This wild fickle wind is your lover,
   And the cloud and the cold are your friends !

SLIGHTED VALUES.

IF diamonds lay thicker than pebbles,
    What plodder would rank them higher?
What searcher would covet their shining,
    Or gather them out of the mire?
They are prized for their rarity only,
    And not for their hearts of fire.

Our greatest blessings are cheapest,
    Costing no toil or pain ;
No miser can heap for increase,
    No usurer hoard for gain,
The gold of the priceless sunshine,
    The gems of the precious rain.

Who measures the blessed daylight,
    And sells us a costly share?
Who doles out the crystal currents
    Which gush for us everywhere,
Or reckons by varying values
    The worth of the vital air?

Yet men are so blind and selfish,
  Their hearts are so hard and cold,
That all things are undervalued
  Which have not their price in gold;
And nothing is reckoned precious
  That cannot be bought and sold.

FAITH AND SIGHT.

IF the Great Ruler of the worlds should be
   Moved to descend from His eternal place,
  To veil the awful splendor of His face
And lay aside invisibility,
So that our feeble eyes unblindedly
   Might bear the softened glory, by His grace,
   How gladly should we hasten to embrace
The privilege of worship at His knee!
  From every corner of earth's peopled space,
From every island shouldered by the sea,
   How would all souls, of every clime and race,
Gather to pour strong prayer and tremulous plea,
   Unuttered now, because we cannot trace
The way to Him, and lack the faith to see!

AN OLD POET.

IF near my dwelling, in the city's maze,
   A silver-throated bird should come and sing,
From dawn till dark, his wild melodious lays,
   Sweeter than thrushes' notes at evening,
   And I should own that his clear carolling

Made all the world more beautiful to me,
   Raising my soul above its paltry cares
Into a region loftier and more free,
   Of purer daylight and diviner airs,
   Until my life grew holier unawares;

If I should listen all the summer long,
   And hoard his warbled wisdom in my breast,
But yield him, in repayment for his song,
   Nor food, nor drink, nor any place of rest,
   Not even straws and mosses for a nest,

And even when the autumn skies grew dim,
    And all the outer world was bare and chill,
Should fail to comfort or to shelter him,
    But only wonder at his feebler trill,
    And smile and listen, smile and listen still,

And when his clear voice reached its saddest chord,
    Should close my eyes in ecstasy, and say,
" The gift of singing is its own reward,"
    And let him sing unfed, day after day,
    Until he sang his starving heart away, —

Would it not be a base and cruel wrong
    To take his best, and give him naught again?
To make my life the richer by his song,
    Yet let him pour his own away in vain,
    And die when winter comes, in want and pain?

Yet so the world deals with its singing-birds.
    Men call them poets; from their airy height
Who sing their precious thoughts in golden words,
    And to our dull lives, dim with mists and blight,
    Send down consoling echoes of delight.

O poet! gentlest friend of humankind!
　Thy rare anointing helps our ears to hear,
Our eyes to see, where we were deaf and blind,
　The myriad chords in Nature's chorus clear,
　The myriad beauties of the changing year!

Thou liftest us, by magic all thine own,
　Above our work-day being's sordid bound,
And leading us by ways we have not known,
　Beyond the dust of life's ignoble round,
　Placest our feet upon enchanted ground!

We say, "The poet joys in singing." So
　We let him sing, and starve. And while he sings,
The summer passes, and the winter's snow
　Whitens his hair, yet no rewarding brings
　To him who gave us eyes and ears and wings.

And if, at last, in grief and penury,
　His soaring voice, but now so clear and bold,
Break, with his heart, we smile indulgently,
　And say among ourselves, "He groweth old,"
　And let him die with hunger, want, and cold.

If even the clown is worthy of his hire,
What earthly gift can be too great for him
Who lights our altars with Promethean fire,
And tunes our souls till through these vapors dim
We almost hear the songs of seraphim?

A FORSAKEN FAVORITE.

THIS world has many types of loneliness :
　　The last leaf, fluttering in November's gale ;
A widowed bird, that sits and calls in vain ;
The empty chair of one we used to love ;
A lighthouse beacon on a stormy night ;
A vacant bird-cage, whence the song has died ;
An autumn rose upon its frosty brier ;
A sea-gull, floating in the winter sky ;
A sweetheart waiting for a recreant love ;
A late star, twinkling faintly into day ;
A ship alone upon the trackless sea ;
A butterfly, belated in a frost ;
A baby's grave upon a western trail ;
A ruined homestead, shone on by the moon.

Yet none seems drearier than the household pet
Once welcomed to the warmest fireside place,
A purring, proud, luxurious favorite,
Which haunts, at evening of a wintry day,

The doorstep of a house untenanted,
From which her false, forgetful friends have gone,
Leaving her homeless, hungry, and forlorn.
Vainly she waits the care she used to know,
The children's call, the evening's milky feast,
The gentle hand that smoothed her furry sides ;
Raises alternately her patient feet,
Benumbed and aching, from the icy stone,
Watches the shuttered windows piteously,
And mews, despairing, at the bolted door.

NATURE'S HEALERS.

THE child lay sick on her tiresome bed;
   Her face was whitened and drawn with pain,
And her mother sorrowed, and sadly said,
While tears fell fast on the golden head,
   " Ah, me, will she ever be well again?"

The bird outside on the window-sill
   Sung loud a joyful and merry strain;
He pecked at the glass with his yellow bill;
He danced, and warbled with glad good-will,
   " Come out-of-doors and be well again!"

The bee plunged in at the open door,
   And beat his forehead against the pane,
Bright were the golden rings he wore;
He buzzed on the ceiling, the wall, the floor,
   And said, " Come out, and be well again!"

The breeze came in at the lifted sash,
    Full of the strength of the sweet salt main;
It told of the brook's soft purl and plash,
Of new-fledged birds in the roadside ash,
    And whispered, "Come and be well again!"

The flowers leaned from their crystal vase;
    They were brought by her mates from dell and plain;
They kissed and fondled her fevered face;
They beckoned and nodded with wooing grace,
    And said, "Arise, and be well again!"

The rain came out of its cloud, and beat
    With dripping fingers against the pane;
And "Come!" it gurgled; "the air is sweet,
There are grassy pools for your burning feet;
    Come out-of-doors and be well again!"

She writhed and moaned in her fever-toss,
    And mocking visions beset her brain;
She dreamed of showers and cool moist moss,
Of clear waves, foaming the ledge across,
    To turn the mill-wheel with might and main.

"Give me your bloom, O flowers," said she;
  "Give me your fresh, sweet breath, O rain;
Give me your vigor, O tireless bee;
Give me your life, O wind of the sea,
  That I may be strong and well again!"

And long ere the forest nuts were browned, —
  When fields were rich with the rustling grain,
And early apples grew red and round, —
Out with the reapers, alert and sound,
  The little maiden was well again!

THE STORY OF KIDHZ.

MOHAMMED of Arabia, a wise man
Surnamed Kazwini, who was born and lived
And wrote and died in the seventh century
Of the Hegira, in his manuscripts
(As from the lips of the immortal Kidhz)
Tells this strange story of the work of time
And everlasting change, to show the might
Of Nature and the ages, and to mark
The littleness and brief estate of man,
Who calls himself the master of the earth,
And thinks all things therein were made for him.

I, Kidhz, who cannot die, walked forth one day
And saw a city, populous and grand,
Built in the middle of a fruitful plain;
Rich were its stately palaces, and tall
Its hundred towers, which glistened in the light;
And to a dweller standing in the gate,
I spake, and said, " It is a goodly place;
How long, I pray thee, has the city stood?"

And he replied, " How strange a man art thou !
Our sires, nor theirs before them, never knew
A time when this great city was not here,
Proud, grand, eternal, as thou seest it;
It hath been always even as it is now."

Five hundred years went by, and once again
I wandered to the splendid city's site;
No vestige of its walls or towers remained, —
The place was one wide stretch of barren clay, —
And, only living thing in all the waste,
A strolling peasant stooped to gather herbs.
" How long," I said, " has this great plain been bare?
What hath destroyed the city that was here?"

And he replied, " Thou ravest, traveller,
No city ever stood on this wide plain;
This is no place for domes and palaces;
Our fathers and our fathers' fathers knew
That it hath always been as it is now."

Five hundred years had passed, when yet once more
I wandered where the arid plain had been;
And lo! the sea rolled there, with waves and ships
And wrecks and rages. On the shingly shore

Among the wave-worn stones and broken shells,
A fisher mended nets. I spake and said,
"When did these waters overflow the land?
How long, I pray thee, has the sea been here?"

"How long?" he said, and mocked me. "Verily,
The sea was always here. My fathers won
Their living from its waters, even as I;
So will my children's children after me.
The sea abides forever. Art thou mad?"

Again five ages passed. I sought the place,
And there was neither city, sand, nor sea,
But one vast, tangled, pathless wilderness,
Where strange beasts roamed, and strange birds built their nests;
And of a lonely hunter I inquired,
"How long has this great forest flourished here,
And where have fled the waters of the sea
Which rolled and murmured when I stood here last?"

"The sea?" he said; "the sea is leagues away.
Thou dreamest, or art merry with much wine;

My fathers and their fathers hunted here
In this great forest, whereof no man knows
The age, because it hath been always here!"

Again five centuries passed, and yet again
I walked that way; and lo! before my eyes
There stood a city, populous and fair,
Richer and statelier than that of old,
Full of all beauty, wisdom, and delight.
And to a loiterer I spake, and said,
"I pray thee, when was this great city built?
Who felled the mighty forest that was here?"

He gazed at me, and fear was in his eyes:
"The city? 'T is indeed an ancient one;
Its generations have grown old and died;
It hath been thus through all recorded time,
And there was never any forest here!"

"A GARDEN ENCLOSED."

SHUT from the dusty way
    Wherein I walk each day,
By a mere paling, only shoulder-high,
    A bit of garden lies
    Unseen by careless eyes,
Yet never missed by mine, as I pass by.

    Though noontide's fervent heat
    Pervade the sandy street,
And scorching pavements render back the glow,
    Freshness and shade abound
    In that enchanted ground,
And cool, sweet odors from its silence flow.

    Even when fierce dog-days
    Send down their hottest blaze,
The air seems moist and soft as early June;
    The leaves, unwilted, keep
    Their crisp, cool, rustling sweep,
And dewdrops linger until afternoon.

Encircled by a crowd
Of flowers, less bright and proud,
The stately foxglove lifts its veinèd bells;
The pansy's brilliant face
Looks up, with quaint grimace,
Out of the cool, damp shadow where it dwells.

There flutter winged sweet-peas,
And larkspurs tempt the bees
With pyramids of purple-petalled bloom;
Lilies seem native there,
And roses balm the air
Where late the lilac waved its perfumed plume.

There nestles mignonette,
Not beautiful, but yet
Holding an inner grace that shuns the sight;
Unnoticed, but content
To please with subtile scent,
And bless the noon with wafts of rare delight,

Proving how poorer far
External beauties are
Than some fine fragrance of the soul may be,
Which, spite of noise and heat,
Makes dusty ways more sweet,
Though few perceive its patient ministry.

But though this paradise
So near the highway lies,
Its beauties bloom unseen by almost all;
The heedless human tide
That ebbs and flows outside,
Sweeps blindly by its bare, brown breadth of wall.

Musing, I sometimes ask,
" Is there, behind the mask
Of those I meet, cold-eyed and blank of face,
A realm enclosed apart,
A noble, tender heart,
Like this shut garden, full of bloom and grace?"

Perhaps their alien eyes
Serve only to disguise
The spirit's beauty, and so wrong it all;
And visions of delight
Would meet my wondering sight,
Could I but look beyond the boundary wall.

FOUR WORDS.

BELOVED, the briefest words are best;
   And all the fine euphonious ways
In which the truth has been expressed
   Since Adam's early Eden days,
   Could never match the simple phrase, —
     Sweetheart, I love you!

If I should say the world were blank
   Without your face; if I should call
The stars to witness, rank on rank,
   That I am true, although they fall, —
   'T would mean but this, — and this means all, —
     Sweetheart, I love you!

And so, whatever change is wrought
   By time or fate, delight or dole,
One single happy, helpful thought
   Makes strong and calm my steady soul,
   And these sweet words contain the whole, —
     Sweetheart, I love you!

I will not wrong their truth to-day
  By wild, impassioned vows of faith,
Since all that volumes could convey
  Is compassed thus in half a breath,
  Which holds and hallows life and death, —
    Sweetheart, I love you!

ALWAYS A BABY.

SHE sat in the summer gloaming
    And talked of the days long past, —
A woman, whose feet were nearing
    Life's sunset shadows fast;

A woman whose form was bending
    Under the weight of years,
Whom seventy summers and winters
    Had touched with their smiles and tears.

Her life had been dimmed by sorrows,
    And changeful with lights and shades,
Yet her heart was fresh with the fountain
    Of a youth that never fades.

She spoke of the cares of a mother,
    Of the labor of heart and hand
Which a group of restless children
    From her patient love demand;

Of the wide fair circle of faces
    Which around her hearth had met;
Of the group of men and women
    Who called her " mother " yet, —

Some of them bold and busy
    In the world's engrossing maze,
While others remained beside her
    To comfort her waning days.

And then she spoke of her first-born,
    With a mother's tender praise, —
A baby, whose little lifetime
    Was reckoned by weeks and days.

But her lashes were bright with tear-drops,
    And her voice was broken and low,
As she spoke of the baby that perished
    Full fifty years ago.

" Were he living," she murmured,
    As a slow tear downward rolled,
" He would be gray and time-worn,
    More than fifty years old.

"Ah, although my living children
    Are loving and fair and brave,
My heart still yearns for my first-born,
    Asleep in his tiny grave,

"Over whose peaceful pillow
    So many seasons have rolled.
Ah, he would be, were he living,
    More than fifty years old!

"I think of him often and often,
    For he, of all my brood,
Stays always a rosy infant,
    Immortal in babyhood."

O wondrous love of the mother,
    Whose marvellous strength and truth
Transfigured her face with a beauty
    Sweeter than that of youth!

O constant heart of the mother,
    So tenderly touched to tears,
After the joys and sorrows
    And changes of fifty years!

REST.

WHEREFORE this bitter aching of the heart
    When our beloved depart,
To whom our souls have grown through years and
    years
    Of toil and tears?

Why weep for those who happily forget
    Life's tedious wear and fret,
Who lay aside, with joy, the loads of ill
    Which cramp us still?

Wash not, O tears, these white and quiet feet
    Which, clean from dust and heat,
Shall climb, through all the round of coming days,
    No more rough ways.

Lave not, O tears, these calmly folded hands
    Slipped from their fettering bands,
Which, whether want would pinch or wrong despoil,
    Know no more toil.

Fall not, O tears, above the pulseless heart
    Forgetful of its smart,
Which shall forever, while the slow years wane,
    Know no more pain.

Drop not upon this fair and peaceful face
    Pure from all earthly trace,
Which shall, through all the cycles of the years,
    Know no more tears.

For ah, it matters not how much we claim
    Of wealth and love and fame;
What boon at last so dear to mortal breast
    As this, — of rest?

THE CLAY CHERUB.

WHAT is immortal? Dreamers speak of love
　　Outliving mortal breath,
And conquering fate and circumstance and death;
And wise men preach, and poets sing in rhyme
Of faith and fame which years cannot disprove,
　　And hope which laughs at time.
And yet the veriest trifles oft outlast
All these, and leave them in the misty past,
Proving how empty is their boast above
A silken shred, a flower, or faded glove.

He took a piece of potter's earth one day, —
　　My friend, remembered still, —
And, with an artist's ready craft and skill,
Fashioned for me a little cherub face.
"Alas!" I said, "why make of brittle clay
　　A thing of so much grace,
So beautiful and sweet and dainty fair?
Its lines will yield to the effacing air
Their delicate curving, shield it as I may,
And dry and crumble, grain by grain, away."

The brows were bent as in a wondering dream,
  Half joy and half surprise;
The gentle lids closed over sleeping eyes;
The tender lips just parted in a smile
So sweet and life-like, it would almost seem
  That in a little while
It would awaken, laughing, from its rest;
And quietly across the baby breast,
Which slumber's lightest breathing seemed to thrill,
Two angel wings were folded, soft and still.

He smiled, and touched the rounded cheek of clay,
  And gravely said to me:
" This little face you prize so tenderly
Holds in itself no element of change,
No germ of dissolution or decay;
  And it would not be strange
If in so kind and loving hands as yours
It lasts for years, and even still endures
When much that you and I, dear child, to-day
Believe immortal, shall have passed away."

How truly did he speak! Death's seal was set
  Even then upon his face,
Though love refused to see its fatal trace;

And though the world was fair with light and bloom,
Still in his eyes, where mirth and feeling met,
   There lay a shade of doom.
Long since, their earnest depths forgot the light;
But wrapped in happy sleep and visions bright,
Unchanged by time, unshadowed by regret,
The little cherub face is perfect yet.

The hand which dowered with life a marble bust,
   And caught a marvellous ray
Of beauty in this bit of worthless clay,
That wrought out power and passion from a stone,
Called smiles from cold Carrara's prisoning crust,
   By skilful touch alone,
Awakened loveliest dimples in a cheek
Rock-hewn, and made the carved lip almost speak,
Has now, oblivious of its lofty trust,
Forgot its cunning, and returned to dust.

In the true heart that loved him, even yet
   The wild and frantic grief
Which long rejected solace and relief,
Has only changed to fixed and silent pain;
And every spring-time, when the violet
   Wakes to the loving rain,

While the glad birds build, and the new leaves grow,
And the brooks sing, its blossom sweet and low
Keeps vigil by his rest, with blue eye wet,
Like one who waits, and never will forget.

What has it not outlived and put to shame,
   Outlasting their decay,
This little fragment of untempered clay?
Youth, love, and all that makes existence dear;
Life's brightest dreams, an artist's dawning fame,
   A woman's hope and fear,
A child's sweet life, that promised to atone
For years of toil and woe endured alone,
Faith's strong reliance, friendship's steadiest flame;
And yet the clay-wrought face remains the same!

Wherefore it seems these trifles, which we call
   Mere nothings of a day,
Last when our soul's best treasures pass away;
Beside the life-time of a book-pressed flower,
Love's fond forever dwindles brief and small,
   And fame is for an hour;
Joy's promise fades before a rose's red,
And clay endures when youth and hope are dead;
Shadows outlast our trust, as years befall,
But human sorrow long outlives them all!

APRIL AGAIN.

WHEN snow lies deep on vale and plain,
    And tempests sweep the shore and main,
How vain and empty seems the knowledge
    That summer-time will come again!

The waiting wood stands gray and dim,
    A waste of rigid trunk and limb,
With yet no hint of coming foliage,
    Of springing flower, or warbler's hymn.

The shrouded garden gives no sign;
    Faintly the pallid sunbeams shine, —
Chill smiles which have no vital meaning,
    On barren shrub and leafless vine.

Not yet, along the last year's bed,
    The fearless crocus lifts its head;
The snow lies deep, and growth and beauty
    Have not yet risen from the dead.

Yet time will vivify it all;
To-day, by yonder trellised wall,
Amid a fruit-tree's naked branches
I heard the welcome bluebird's call.

What cared he, though beneath his eye
The snowy drifts lay wide and high?
He knew he wore, on neck and pinion,
The sapphire of the summer sky.

Unsleeping Nature never errs,
Nor once forgets what she defers;
The red buds greaten on the maples,
As in their veins the sweet blood stirs;

And toward the sun, which kindlier burns,
The earth, awaking, looks and yearns,
And still, as in all other Aprils,
The annual miracle returns.

Dearer than summer's pageantry,
Or autumn's glow on land and sea,
Is spring's sweet time of hope and promise,
When all things fair are yet to be!

THE FOG.

FROM the ocean depths below,
   With their shadows of amethyst,
     In the mystical morning light,
     She rises, the goddess white,
   With her legions of wreathing mist,
And banners of pearl and snow.

With never a curb or rein
   Does the gleaming goddess ride
     Her courser of silver gray.
     See, whiter than beaten spray,
   The breath of his nostrils wide,
The toss of his flying mane!

Her legions follow behind
   In a dim and shifting crowd;
     Formless, obscure, and slow,
     They gather and rise and go,
   Like ghosts in a pallid shroud,
In the van of the waking wind.

They thicken the humid air;
　　They curtain the sea and land;
　　　　They follow her lightest beck,
　　　　The curve of her courser's neck,
　　The wave of her lifted hand,
The trail of her drifting hair.

Swift after their moving cloud
　　The screaming sea-birds flock;
　　　　As the hurrying squadrons haste,
　　　　Afar in the lonesome waste,
　　The sea-lion, from his rock,
To the misty host calls loud.

Gone, in a dim white whirl
　　Over the sun-waked sea;
　　　　A fluttering silver veil
　　　　Flies back on the rising gale.
　　Who governs their flight but she,
With her sceptre of snow and pearl?

LOYALTY.

THIS rose which makes my chamber sweet,
    Cream-white, and full of rare perfume,
Defies the chill December day,
    And makes a summer in my room;
For this one blossom signifies
    The whole fair tropic's wealth of bloom.

But should some cold-eyed critic come
    To scan its snowy blossoming,
Saying, " It is but faint and poor
    To those which summer-time will bring;
Why linger with delighted eyes
    Above the pale, imperfect thing ? "

If this should be, would it destroy
    My rose's bloom and scent for me?
Would my fond eyes grow dim or blind
    Because another's could not see
The charm which bowers my wintry room
    With summer's leafy luxury?

Ah, no! my rose would still be white,
    Its odor still transport my sense;
And gazing in its golden heart,
    My soul would find sweet recompense
For all the outside world's decay,
    And all the beauty vanished thence.

Thus do I hold you, friend beloved:
    My heart perceives you good and true;
My eyes behold you proud and brave,
    With soul and eyes as clear as dew;
And all the envious tongues on earth
    Could never change my love for you.

And other friends might stand afar,
    Or cease to speak your once-loved name;
And all the world might pass you by,
    Or all the world might chide or blame,
It would not make me deaf or blind;
    And I should love you all the same!

THE SWALLOWS.

From the French of Pierre de Béranger.

HELD captive on the Moorish shore,
 A soldier sighed beneath his chain;
"O swallows, ye have come once more!
 With joy I mark your flight again.
Tender hopes have followed you
 Even to this burning strand,
From the France which once I knew;
 Tell me of my native land!
  Birds of home! ye know so well,
  Tell me, swallows, tell me of my country, tell!

"Three years have ye not heard my prayer?
 O swallows, bring me if ye may
Some tidings of the valley where
 I dreamed my youthful years away!
By a winding stream serene,
 Bowered by lilacs sweet and pale,
Oft our cottage ye have seen;
 Tell me of that happy vale!
  Birds of home! ye know so well,
  Tell me, swallows, tell me of our cottage, tell!

"Mayhap beneath its mossy eaves
    Your life, as well as mine, begun.
You know how sore my mother grieves
    And yearns to clasp the absent one.
Long she listens, but in vain,
    Sounds of my returning feet,
Hearkens, weeps, and waits again
    The wanderer to greet.
        Birds of home! ye know so well,
        Tell me, swallows, all her love and sorrow, tell!

"Companion of my childish play, —
    My sister, — is she yet a bride?
And did our lads make glad the day,
    With wedding songs of joy and pride?
Ah, those youthful friends of yore,
    Have they ceased with war to roam?
Do they see our vale once more,
    Our dear old village home?
        Birds of France! ye know so well,
        Tell me, swallows, tell me of my comrades, tell!

"Perhaps a rude invading throng
    Exult their fallen forms above,
And load with deep and bitter wrong
    The helpless objects of my love.

Ah, no more my mother's prayer
  Shall I hear arise for me!
Weary fetters I must wear
  In this far captivity.
    Birds of France! ye know so well,
    Tell me, swallows, tell me of my country, tell!"

A WINTER GRAVE.

WHEN in the soft and gracious summer weather,
    Some tired soul passes, and a grave is made,
How soon, by growing grass-roots laced together,
    The sods forget the wounding of the spade!

For Nature rallies all her subtile forces,
    Wind, sunshine, and the growth-compelling rain;
And ere a score of days have run their courses,
    The scars are healed, the turf is green again.

And though our sorrow fills the utmost measure,
    Some sweetness mingles with its bitterest part;
We know how tenderly our buried treasure
    Is folded close in Nature's mother-heart.

The soft brown mould is neither cold nor cruel;
    Among its grass what loving fancies grow!
The common flower that holds its dewdrop jewel
    Seems conscious of the gentle heart below.

But when the frozen ground is forced asunder
   In winter-time, by long and patient toil,
That some dear head may find its resting under
   The heavy silence of the unwilling soil,

How cruel seems the earth, which will not render
   One summer scent, one blade of grass, or leaf!
Even Nature's self seems careless and untender,
   And adds another pang to aching grief.

Weary indeed must be the heart to covet
   The chilly rest beneath the frozen ground;
No humblest weed or bramble bends above it,
   No songster warbles near the lonesome mound.

Yet though to-day no loving blossom raises
   Its hopeful face above the wintry tomb,
The icy sods are full of sleeping daisies,
   Which wait but spring, to wake to life and bloom.

THROUGH THE WHEAT.

ONCE, when my heart and I were young,
    We wandered, restless, by sea and strand,
And lingered a little space among
    The sheltered valleys of Switzerland, —

Where watchful summits forever frown
    Through blue air slanting clear and keen,
Wearing proudly their icy crown,
    While happiest hamlets smile between;

Where rapid torrents, rejoicing, run,
    Leaping the cliffs in strength and pride,
Like snow-white ribbons in wind and sun
    Fluttering down the mountain-side;

Where smoke-like cloudings of tender blue
    Dapple the slopes in the sunnier spots,
And sweetly change, on a nearer view,
    To drifts of fairest forget-me-nots.

Often at eve, when the sun was low
    And the mountain shadows grew dark and vast,
I watched the cottagers, wending slow
    Home to rest when their toil was past.

Two walked lovingly, side by side,
    Speaking softly as lovers speak, —
He with an air of manly pride,
    She with a blush on her sun-browned cheek.

Hand in hand through the evening red
    They went, in the shadows moist and sweet,
Choosing a narrow path that led
    On and on through the growing wheat.

Sunset touched him with rosy light;
    Sunset brightened her loosened hair.
Poor and plain, they were fair to sight,
    For youth and love are forever fair.

And often, when sunset charms the air,
    For the time and scene are vanished now,
I think of that simple loving pair,
    And wonder whether they kept their vow;

Whether under some mossy roof,
   Their wedded spirits serenely blent,
They weave the even warp and woof
   Of their quiet being in calm content,

Or whether they parted in scorn and wrath,
   As myriad lovers have done before,
And choosing each a separate path,
   Were thence divided forevermore;

Or whether still, as across the land
   The dewy shadows grow damp and sweet,
Perennial lovers, with hand in hand,
   They walk knee-deep in the growing wheat.

STORM.

IF this November storm, that grieves
   Among the dripping trees to-night,
Would only moan of fallen leaves
   And frosted flowers and wintry blight,

Would speak in plaintive prophecy
   Of coming dearth and cold alone,
It might be borne, for there would be
   Regret, not heart-ache, in its tone.

But ah, it tells of sadder things
   Than Nature's gloomiest moods impart,
And in its mournful minor, sings
   The hidden woes of every heart.

And as the wild wind sobs and cries,
   Long-silent voices speak again;
Dim ghosts of buried sorrows rise
   To haunt us with the olden pain.

O Love, who, though the June departs,
   Keepest thy summer sweet and warm,
Stand thou between our homesick hearts
   And this unkind November storm!

VACANT PLACES.

HOW much soever in this life's mutations
    We seek our shattered idols to replace,
Not one, in all the myriads of the nations,
    Can ever fill another's vacant place.

Each has his own, the smallest and most humble,
    As well as he revered the wide world through;
At every death some loves and hopes must crumble,
    Which never strive to build themselves anew.

If the fair race of violets should perish
    Before another spring-time has its birth,
Could all the costly blooms which florists cherish
    Bring back its April beauty to the earth?

Not the most gorgeous flower that uncloses
    Could give the olden grace to vale and plain;
Not even Persia's gardens full of roses
    Could ever make our world so fair again.

And so with souls we love; they pass and leave us.
　　Time teaches patience at a bitter cost;
Yet all the new loves which the years may give us
　　Fill not the heart-place aching for the lost.

New friends may come to us with spirits rarer,
　　And kindle once again the tear-drowned flame;
But yet we sigh, " This love is stronger, fairer,
　　And better, it may be; but not the same!"

A PILLOW OF ROSES.

MY home is afar from the town and its jar,
    Where cool country breezes are blowing;
Where birds, unafraid, warble soft in the shade,
    And beauty and bounty are growing.
No flatterers woo me, no lovers pursue,
    So peace in my cottage reposes;
My days glide along like the flow of a song,
    And I dream on a pillow of roses;
        Ah, never a sleep is so balmy and deep,
           No eyelid so happily closes,
        As hers who lies down without kingdom or crown
           To dream on a pillow of roses!

The fur of the ermine is costly and rare,
    And royalty claims it to robe her;
And buoyant as air are the gossamers fair
    That silver the grass in October;
But neither would spread so delightful a bed
    To solace the world-weary comer,
As roses, which grew in the sunshine and dew,
    And stole all the sweet of the summer.

>   Ah, never a sleep is so balmy and deep,
>   No eyelid so happily closes,
>   As hers who lies down without kingdom or crown
>   To dream on a pillow of roses!

The down of the eider is dainty and soft
  In her nest by the boreal billow,
By covetous mariners plundered too oft
  For a monarch's luxurious pillow;
But the rest of a queen is not always serene,
  And a king upon thorns oft reposes;
How gladly they 'd lay down the sceptre to-day
  To dream on my pillow of roses!
>   Ah, never a sleep is so balmy and deep,
>   No eyelid so happily closes,
>   As hers who lies down without kingdom or crown
>   To dream on a pillow of roses!

THE END.

www.ingramcontent.com/pod-product-compliance
Lightning Source LLC
Chambersburg PA
CBHW030350170426
43202CB00010B/1324